PRIMARY SOURCES OF REVOLUTIONARY SCIENTIFIC DISCOVERIES AND THEORIES™

COPERNICUS AND MODERN ASTRONOMY

JOSH SAKOLSKY

rosen central

Primary Source™

The Rosen Publishing Group, Inc., New York

To Cake—loving you is easy

Published in 2005 by The Rosen Publishing Group, Inc.
29 East 21st Street, New York, NY 10010

First Edition

Library of Congress Cataloging-in-Publication Data

Sakolsky, Josh.
Copernicus and modern astronomy / by Josh Sakolsky.
    p. cm. — (Primary sources of revolutionary scientific discoveries and theories)
Includes bibliographical references and index.
ISBN 1-4042-0305-2 (lib. bdg.)
1. Copernicus, Nicolaus, 1473-1543—Juvenile literature. 2. Astronomers—Poland—Biography—Juvenile literature. 3. Astronomy—Juvenile literature.
I. Title. II. Series.
QB36.C8S35 2004
520'.92—dc22

                2004011296

Printed in Hong Kong

On the cover: Painting by Matejko Jan entitled *Copernicus at Work*, done in 1873.

On the back cover: Top to bottom: Nicolaus Copernicus, Charles Darwin, Edwin Hubble, Johannes Kepler, Gregor Mendel, Dmitry Mendeleyev, Isaac Newton, James Watson *(right)* and Francis Crick *(left)*.

CONTENTS

INTRODUCTION

Have you ever looked up at the night sky and wondered why the stars seem to wheel around Earth? Do you ever wonder why the Sun rises and sets the way that it does or why a year is 365.25 days long?

Modern humans have long been fascinated with the stars and what exactly makes up the universe. In the 1930s, Albert Einstein developed his theory of relativity, which reshaped the way people saw the universe.

MAPPING THE HEAVENS

In the late 1950s, the United States and Russia engaged in a costly race to see which country could put the first object and then person into orbit in outer space. In 1957, Russia beat the United States when the first human-made satellite, *Sputnik I*, orbited Earth. In 1961, Russian cosmonaut Yury Gagarin became the first human being to orbit Earth. While these events had great political significance, they had an even greater impact on the history of humankind. For the first time, humans were in a position to explore space in greater detail.

Today, the Hubble telescope sits in orbit around Earth and collects images from thousands of light-years away. The telescope opened up a window into what is happening in the farthest reaches of the universe. Because the light that produces these pictures also took thousands of light-years to reach

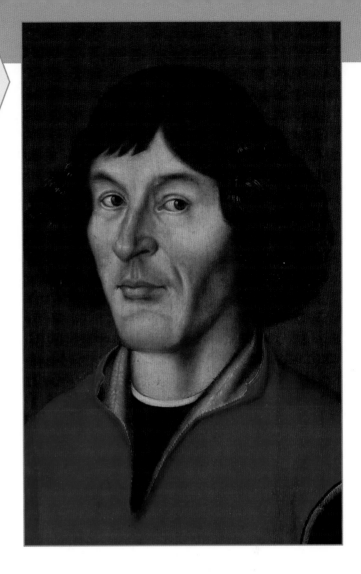

Polish astronomer Nicolaus Copernicus led the way during the first days of the scientific revolution. Copernicus's earth-shaking heliocentric system of the universe posited that the Sun, not Earth, is the center of the universe. For hundreds of years, it was held that Earth is the center of the universe. Copernicus's work to challenge beliefs inspired a long line of great minds that changed the world. From Copernicus to Galileo to Isaac Newton to Albert Einstein, great minds have contributed to science and allowed humankind to have a better understanding of the universe.

Earth, the resulting images allow scientists to examine the beginnings of time itself. Now, astrophysicists (scientists who study the physics of the universe) can "see" almost back to the point when the universe began.

The attempt to answer these question as to how the universe began and to address humankind's role in it, however, is as old as human history itself. The ancient civilizations of Greece, Babylonia, Egypt, as well as many others, all attempted to construct an order to the heavens that would explain humankind's place and role in the universe. The theories from these ancient astronomers were not always based on facts derived from astronomical observations. Most of these cosmologies had religious elements that were extremely important to keeping their respective societies prosperous and functioning. For example, the ancient Egyptians believed that Earth was shaped similar to a serving platter with a lid of air in a dome shape serving as the home of the stars and other planets. The Sun, known as the god Ra, traveled across this dome. When he dipped below the horizon, the day was over. Furthermore, because Egyptian agriculture was heavily dependent on the flooding of the Nile River, Egyptians developed a calendar that had an equal number of days in each month (thirty). However, because they discovered that this created inaccuracies, they added five festival days to the end of the last month so that the calendar would remain accurate from year to year and keep the cycles of the Nile floods consistent. This system, used to explain the mysteries of the universe, fit the Egyptians' needs in terms of record keeping and agricultural practices, as well as their religious beliefs, so they saw no reason to improve upon it.

Thousands of years later, that very understanding of the universe would be challenged by Nicolaus Copernicus, a Polish astronomer who lived during the Renaissance. The Renaissance was a period of great awakening in art and culture lasting from the early 1400s to the late 1600s in Europe. It was also a time when scholars and philosophers rediscovered and reinterpreted the thinking of ancient civilizations. Through his many years of astronomical observations and mathematical calculations, Copernicus came up with a system for the known universe that put the Sun at its center. This heliocentric, or sun-centered, universe was a radical change from the accepted structure of the universe. Copernicus's heliocentric system would eventually become the building block for other astronomers to create an accurate map of the heavens. It was his willingness to challenge the accepted wisdom of his age that led Copernicus to come up with his earth-shaking model of the universe. This radical new idea would displace humans from their station at the supreme point of creation. Copernicus's work would eventually prove that Earth is not the center of the universe.

Copernicus's work was so great a challenge to the accepted authorities, such as the leaders of Catholic Church and other established scholars of astronomy, that Copernicus kept his ideas to himself for years. He was worried that his ideas would be rejected and that they would become the object of ridicule and be dismissed by other astronomers. It was his love of learning and belief in the principles of scientific observation that gave him the courage to eventually have his work published for the whole world to see. At first, some of his deepest concerns were realized: for years after his work was published, his ideas were rejected by the leaders of the Catholic Church. However, later scientists such as Johannes Kepler and Galileo Galilei built on his ideas, and from his foundation, helped turn astronomy into a modern science.

CHAPTER 1

EARLY LIFE AND EDUCATION

Nicolaus Copernicus was born on February 19, 1473, in the town of Torun, Poland (which was then known as Royal Prussia). His father, also named Nicolaus, was a successful merchant whose career started in Kraków, Poland, where he gained a reputation as a trustworthy and effective trader. Sometime in the 1460s, the elder Nicolaus moved to Torun and began courting Barbara Watzenrode, the daughter of a prominent family in town. This led to marriage and the eventual birth of the younger Nicolaus along with his brother and two sisters.

Located on the Vistula River, Torun was a prosperous trading town in the late Middle Ages and was part of the kingdom of Poland. This kingdom of Poland was smaller than today's Poland, and many of its inhabitants spoke German instead of Polish as their primary language. Torun was considered a thriving city during the Middle Ages, with a population of nearly 20,000. The city was a cultural center with a

Copernicus's home in Torun, Poland, still stands some 500 years after his birth. Copernicus's father was a wealthy businessman and a respected town leader. When Copernicus was ten years old, his father died, and Copernicus went to live with his uncle Lucas Watzenrode, a church canon. There, Copernicus began a career in the church. Both his brother and two sisters would later gain posts in the church. Today, Torun is home to Nicolaus Copernicus University.

9

rich and interesting history. Founded in the late thirteenth century, the town had come to dominate the river trade and was always bustling with merchants. However, the city had also seen its share of turmoil and strife. At the time, Torun was under the influence of the Order of Teutonic Knights, a powerful group of soldiers who controlled most of the land around the town. For years, the leaders of the order sought to take Torun from the king of Poland and rule it for themselves. Torun's leaders eventually formed a coalition, or organization, with other nearby towns in the same situation to keep out the Order of Teutonic Knights. About ten years before Copernicus's birth, this coalition succeeded and the Teutonic Knights were forced to leave these towns alone.

As a young boy with newfound freedoms, Nicolaus probably had many opportunities to wander the streets of Torun and enjoy the various cultures and people who flocked to his city. Since Torun is a port city, Nicolaus would have also heard sailors and merchants talking of their travels. These tales may have awakened in him a desire to see the world outside his native lands.

At age ten, however, Nicolaus's father died of unknown causes. Fortunately, Nicolaus's uncle, Lucas Watzenrode, watched over young Nicolaus. Watzenrode was an important man in the Catholic Church and would later become bishop of Warmia in 1489. Watzenrode made sure that Nicolaus was able to get an education, most likely at the Studium Particulare, which was an academically rigorous grammar school located in the neighboring town of Chelmno. It was here that Nicolaus probably began his studies in Latin. At the time, Latin was the

Formed at the end of the twelfth century, the Order of Teutonic Knights was a crusading group of knights under the guidance of the Roman Catholic Church. In the early part of the fifteenth century, the Teutonic Knights began to lose power with the rise of Poland. This painting captures the fury of the Teutonic Knights during one of its crusades to recapture parts of the Holy Land in the Middle East.

international language of scholars and educated people. Watzenrode's early willingness to take responsibility for his nephew's education would blossom into lifelong patronage, providing help and vital economic support for Nicolaus.

ASTRONOMY DURING THE MIDDLE AGES

Astronomy during the Middle Ages mostly involved observing the sky with the naked eye. A few crude tools had been developed, allowing astronomers to measure the angles between themselves and the object they were looking at. They could also measure the angles between stars or other astronomical bodies. They applied these measurements to the theories of geometry that had come

down to them from writings of the ancient Greeks that had been preserved by monks and Islamic scholars. Astronomers at this time also sought to find lost works and publish them. Through this combination of scholarship and observation, astronomers believed they could finally perfect the planetary system of Ptolemy, an ancient Egyptian astronomer who put Earth at the center of the universe.

During medieval times, astronomy was slow to develop in Europe. However, in the Arab world, astronomy was quickly progressing. Islamic astronomer Al-Farghani wrote about the movement of celestial bodies in the tenth century. A century later, an enormous observatory was built near Tehran, Iran. When Copernicus proposed his heliocentric theory, Europeans quickly turned to studying the heavens.

Off to Kraków

After years of primary schooling that increased his appetite for more learning, Nicolaus enrolled in the University of Kraków at the age of nineteen. Located in the capital of the

Polish kingdom, this was arguably the finest institution of higher education in all of eastern Europe. The university also had an especially strong reputation among scholars as a seat of mathematical and astronomical learning. Kraków was home to an international community of scholars and there was a buzz of various languages spoken by students, teachers, and merchants in the bustling city. Copernicus would have greatly enjoyed this cosmopolitan atmosphere.

Among the many well-respected mathematicians and astronomers with whom Nicolaus may have studied was Wojciech of Brudzewo. This highly learned man came to Kraków during the term of 1491 to 1492. Wojciech not only gave lectures at the university, but also taught in private settings where he was able to work closely with his more talented pupils. Although it is not known if Nicolaus attended any of these private sessions, one would not be surprised if he had. By this time, Nicolaus's mind was already turning toward the heavens, and was probably seeking out great minds in astronomy. After all, it was while he was in Kraków that Nicolaus purchased and had bound together two important astronomy books. One book, complete with Copernicus's signature on the cover page, still exists today in a library in Sweden and contains the second printed edition of the *Alfonsine Tables* and the *Tables of Directions*. Both of these were fundamental texts used by astronomers at this time. The *Alfonsine Tables* was a collection of astronomical data, named for King Alfonso X of Castille, Spain, who had it published in the late thirteenth century. The book, which was compiled by more than fifty astronomers, was full of astronomical observations that could be used for further calculations by future astronomers as a sort of blueprint. It provided the raw information that any

The world was going through many drastic changes during Copernicus's age. One change was the duel between religion and science. Many age-old beliefs—those often upheld by the Catholic Church—were beginning to be challenged. The life of Copernicus is a perfect example of this struggle. He devoted much of his early life to religious studies. However, the later part of his life was devoted to science. This photograph captures the very room where Copernicus studied in 1502. By that time, Copernicus was leaving his religious studies and turning toward astronomy.

astronomer needed when working on a problem. Johann Müller (1436–1476), a prominent astronomer from the generation before Copernicus, wrote and published many astronomical books, including the *Tables of Directions*.

Nicolaus's time in Kraków would have a deep influence on his career. His deep study of mathematics while at the university gave him a foundation that he would use when developing his later planetary systems. Also, it is very likely that at this time, he was given instruction on how to make astronomical observations.

In 1495, Nicolaus left Kraków without receiving his degree and traveled to Frombork, Poland (then East Prussia), where he began his duties as a canon of the Frombork cathedral about a year later. Most likely, he left his studies to defend his right to hold this seat, since two other people had appealed to church authorities that they should hold the post. Copernicus was probably placed in the position by his uncle, who had been recently appointed as a bishop, as a way of securing his nephew's economic future. The job as a canon would have supplied Nicolaus with guaranteed income. However, Nicolaus could not settle down for long. Later that year, he left Frombork and headed to Italy to get a law degree from the University of Bologna.

CHAPTER 2

THE WORLD OF ASTRONOMY PRIOR TO COPERNICUS

What would Nicolaus Copernicus have learned about astronomy during his four years of studying in Kraków? Some of the most important sources of astronomy during the Middle Ages were the writings of the ancient Greek philosophers. In the ancient world, philosophers thought about questions of ethics, morals, and politics concerning their societies. In addition, these great minds also debated how the world worked and discussed the elements of natural history. They even performed basic science experiments. However, they still mixed religion with their scientific thinking, believing that the stars, planets, and Sun represented divine objects.

In the Middle Ages, and later during the Renaissance, the most respected of these ancient philosophers were Plato, Eudoxus, Aristotle, and Ptolemy. While other Greek philosophers also developed alternative theories and ideas regarding the heavens and Earth, they never became as popular or widespread enough to displace the thinking of these four.

Astrology is a system of understanding the universe by interpreting the movement of stars, the Sun, and the Moon. In ancient times, astrology was often used to predict or explain the inexplicable, from the weather to human affairs. Astrologers used different constellations, or groups of stars, represented by the twelve different signs of the zodiac. This is an illuminated manuscript page from Ptolemy's *Tetrabiblos*, written in the second century AD. By using the zodiac, Ptolemy attempted to predict the outcome of certain individuals' lives. Centuries later, after the emergence of the scientific method, astrology would be all but discredited, and astronomy would emerge as the credible science of the heavens.

Plato: The Rationalist

Plato was born in 428 BC and died around 348 BC. He was a great thinker on many diverse subjects, including politics, the role of literature and poetry in society, and, of course, natural history and the composition of the universe. For example, in his dialogue, or writing, *Timeaus*, he sought to explain the true character of the universe's origins, arguing that it had been created by some unnamed maker. Plato's ideas on the nature of heavenly bodies influenced astronomers of Copernicus's time. One of the most important of Plato's writings, *Timeaus* dealt with the nature of planetary motion and the actual structure of the universe.

Another important idea that Plato made popular was that the Moon does not shine due to its own light. At the time, Greeks believed that the Moon emitted its own light, much like the Sun does. Anaxagoras, another Greek philosopher who died shortly before Plato's birth, first developed the theory that the Moon actually reflected the Sun's light. He discovered this fact while making observations to explain the reason for lunar eclipses. Anaxagoras concluded that it was Earth blocking the Sun's light from hitting the Moon that caused eclipses, and thus the Moon did not project light on its own. In his book *Cratylus*, Plato defended Anaxagoras's theory and argued so strongly for its truth that it became accepted. It was Plato's reputation as a rational and excellent philosophical thinker that made his argument for the truth of Anaxagoras so persuasive.

Plato would go on to develop other ideas that would have great influence on later European scholars of astronomy. One of these ideas was his belief that Earth rested at the center of the universe. It did not move, but sat perfectly motionless. The Sun was the next object in the heavens, and it was in orbit around Earth. Furthermore, because Plato believed that the planets represented divine objects, he maintained that they must move in a perfect and uniform manner. Plato concluded that this movement was a perfectly circular motion at a constant speed. This theory, however, did not match what happened when one observed the motions of the planets over time. When observed over a period of several nights, the planets appear to speed up and actually move forward and backward across the sky in a looping motion. This is known as retrograde (backward) motion. However, Plato was sure that there was a mathematical solution that would bring this apparent contradiction into line with his theory of the universe. The scholars at the Academy, a school founded by Plato, would wrestle with this challenge over the coming centuries.

Eudoxus, Aristotle, and Planetary Spheres

The Greek mathematician Eudoxus (circa 408–circa 377 BC), who was a student of Plato's, was the first to develop a mathematical solution that fit Plato's theory of the universe and planetary motion. In Eudoxus's model, each of the five other known planets (Mercury, Venus, Mars, Jupiter, and Saturn), moved on the equators of their individual spheres. He then put Earth at the center. Each planetary sphere was nested in three other spheres. A large sphere connected to all of these. This final sphere

MISSED CLUES

As both Anaxagoras and Plato sought to prove that the Moon reflects light, some of the evidence used could have been an important clue to solving another age-old question: is the Earth round or flat? While observing a lunar eclipse, Anaxagoras failed to catch Earth's round shadow on the Moon. Earth's round shadow would have proved that Earth was indeed round! Answering that riddle would take the work of Aristotle, Plato's most brilliant student.

Plato's Academy, located in Athens, Greece, opened around 357 BC and was devoted to philosophy, law, and science. Plato's school fostered some of the greatest minds in the Western world, including Aristotle. Plato would spend the last years of his life at the Academy, instructing everyone from fellow philosophers to future emperors.

contained the stars and rotated so that they also moved from east to west across the sky. The whole point of this bulky model was to find a structure that agreed with Plato's statement that Earth was stationary at the center of the universe, while explaining the apparent motion of the planets that seemed to contradict this.

Each planet required these four spheres to explain its motion around Earth, meaning that the universe had twenty spheres. However, Eudoxus believed that the Moon needed only three spheres to explain its motion, while the Sun also only needed three. The section of the sky holding all the stars, which was called the vault of heaven, was a single sphere. All these groups of spheres rotated around Earth, but none of them were linked to each other. Basically, Eudoxus imagined a model for each planet's motion, but never linked them together in a comprehensive system.

Aristotle (384–322 BC) was also a student of Plato's who believed that any explanation for the structure of the universe must fit together in some connected system that explained the motion of each part in relation to all the other parts in the system. Thus, like gears working together in a machine, when the spheres of one planet turned, they had an effect on the motion of the other planets' spheres. Therefore, to counteract this influence, Aristotle added even more spheres to his system of the universe, eventually coming up with fifty-five spheres. This "mechanical" version of the universe would be held as an authority for many centuries until another philosopher and astronomer, Ptolemy, developed an entirely new system.

Ptolemy

Ptolemy was an Egyptian of Greek descent who lived during the first and second centuries AD. While his writings and work

German mathematician Andreas Cellarius created this engraving, which depicts the Ptolemaic universe, in 1661. Ptolemy (AD circa 85–165) put forth that Earth, being the heaviest of all known planets, is the center of the universe. Different spheres, each with fixed stars, rotated around Earth each day. This system would be widely accepted for more than fifteen centuries.

influenced the world for centuries, little is known about his life. When Ptolemy developed his theory of the universe's structure, he built on prior theories developed by Plato, Eudoxus, and Aristotle. Ptolemy's system was based on a series of geometric ideas regarding the nature of motion around a circle. This motion had to go in a uniform direction and at a constant speed.

In Ptolemy's system, all planetary bodies, as well as the Sun, revolved around Earth in uniform, circular, motions. This is called a geocentric, or Earth-centered, universe. Ptolemy published his work and findings in an enormous volume entitled the *Almagest*. Ptolemy's geocentric theory would be accepted throughout the world for centuries to come.

Authority of the Church

In the fifth century AD, the Roman Catholic Church finally became the dominant Christian sect in western Europe. The

ARISTARCHUS OF SAMOS

Greek astronomer Aristarchus lived in the third century BC and was a mathematician and philosopher. Building on the work of earlier mathematicians, Aristarchus developed a heliocentric, or sun-centered, universe. Aristarchus stated that Earth turned on its own axis as it revolved around a stationary sun. This relationship between Earth and the Sun, Aristarchus claimed, would produce Earth's day-night cycle and the solar year. He also kept the stars in a fixed place in the heavens, surrounding Earth and the Sun.

Although Aristarchus developed a heliocentric universe, his ideas never really gained any support among philosophers and astronomical scholars, and by the Middle Ages, Aristarchus was completely forgotten. Edward Rosen, a historian of astronomy, notes in his book, *Copernicus and the Scientific Revolution*, that it is almost certain that Copernicus was not very familiar with the ideas of Aristarchus and that they had no influence on his own development of a heliocentric universe.

leaders of the church found a good deal in Ptolemy's writing that fit in with Catholic teachings, especially the idea that everything revolved around Earth. The Catholic Church adapted Ptolemy's beliefs to mesh with those of the Bible and, therefore, gave his teachings a favored place in western Europe. As the Catholic Church gained more and more status and power throughout Europe, it became very hard for anyone to challenge these ideas supported by the church.

The Roman Empire and the Middle Ages

The people of the city of Rome, located in central Italy, developed a strong and influential culture. Over time, Rome conquered the rest of Italy and then created an empire from the rest of Europe and parts of Asia. In fact, Ptolemy wrote while living under the control of the Roman Empire. However, in 476 AD, the Roman Empire collapsed after the last wave of crushing barbarian invasions from Germanic tribes. With no central government keeping order, western Europe plunged into a period of chaos known as the Middle Ages, which lasted until about 1500. Most knowledge

The scientific revolution, which sparked earth-shaking revelations such as Copernicus's heliocentric system, was not the only thing to emerge from the Middle Ages. The Renaissance, which began in fourteenth-century Italy, brought with it an immense awakening in art and culture. Prior to the Renaissance, little progress was made in science or art, and these two worlds had nearly ground to a halt. Renaissance artists, such as Michelangelo, Donatello, and Botticelli (his *La Primavera* is above), would inspire and influence artists and thinkers alike for centuries to come.

from the ancient world, such as the astronomical writings of the ancient Greeks, became harder and harder to preserve. Between the chaos resulting from no governmental order and the loss of knowledge from earlier times, these times also became known as the Dark Ages.

One group of people who tried to keep this knowledge available were monks living in monasteries, or religious groups, throughout Europe. They copied as many manuscripts as they could find that held the wisdom of the Greeks and Romans. Unfortunately, because of all the turmoil, many works were still lost. Europe's Dark Ages ended with the dawn of the Renaissance, a period of great awakening. Italy and France became hotbeds of artistic and intellectual achievement, and art and literature emerged from the finest minds in Europe. From these artistic pursuits arose many intellectual challenges, seemingly confronting every belief held over from the Dark Ages. Some minds turned toward politics or discovering new lands. Still, many minds turned toward the sciences, which produced many inventions, including the compass, the telescope, and the printing press. Astronomy, or the study of the heavens, also emerged. With it, people began challenging age-old beliefs. One challenged belief was that of the geocentric universe. It would take the mind of Nicolaus Copernicus to challenge this belief and show the world the true nature of our universe.

CHAPTER 3

opernicus arrived in Bologna, Italy, sometime late in 1496, and enrolled in the University of Bologna as a student of canon law. This was primarily to please his uncle, Bishop Watzenrode, who had also earned a law degree there. Bologna was a rich and prosperous city with one of Europe's oldest universities. It was famous for its law school. It also had many German-speaking students, with whom Copernicus made friends. In 1498, when his older brother, Andrew, arrived in the city to begin his legal studies as well, Copernicus had someone else to share with him the wonders of the city and its rich history.

FURTHER STUDIES AND A BREAKTHROUGH

Copernicus and the Mentor

Although law was not necessarily Copernicus's first love, his enrollment in law school entitled him to take classes anywhere else in the university that he wished. This allowed him to continue to pursue his interest in astronomy and mathematics. He sought out Domenico Maria da Novara, the university's professor of astronomy who had begun to publish challenging and original ideas regarding astronomy. For example, in 1489, da Novara published a book declaring that

Nearly 1,000 years after they were first built, the Tower of Garisenda and the Tower of Asinelli still highlight the Bologna, Italy, cityscape. The Tower of Asinelli rises 330 feet (100 m), and is still open to the public to climb its 498 steps. The Tower of Garisenda, however, is closed due to its tilt of nearly 9 feet (3 m), seemingly defying gravity. While his stay in Bologna was relatively short, it undoubtedly had an immediate impact on the young Copernicus. While in the city, he met Domenico Maria da Novara, an esteemed astronomer. Da Novara's influence would inspire Copernicus in his own scientific pursuits.

Ptolemy, long considered the foremost authority on Earth's geography, had incorrectly calculated the latitudes of most of Europe's cities. Da Novara concluded that these latitudes were actually up to one degree and ten minutes greater than Ptolemy laid out in his *Geography* some twelve centuries earlier. For da Novara, this indicated a shift in the direction of the tilt of Earth's axis. Da Novara also concluded that Earth did not stand still, but instead rotated on its own axis. Da Novara's exact calculations would eventually be proven wrong. However, he would have a profound impact on Copernicus. Through da Novara's actions, Copernicus learned that it was possible to publicly challenge long-held beliefs, such as those put forth by Ptolemy and supported by the Catholic Church.

Because students at the university roomed in private lodgings, Copernicus soon secured a room in professor da Novaro's house. This gave him a chance to work more closely with the professor and gain his respect. A student of Copernicus's, Rheticus, wrote in 1540 that Copernicus said that his knowledge of astronomy was so strong at this time that da Novara considered him, "not so much the pupil as the assistant and witness of the observations."

First Observations

On the evening of March 9, 1497, Copernicus, along with da Novara, recorded that the Moon occulted, or appeared to cut in front of and hide the star Aldebaran. This was the first known astronomical observation made by Copernicus. Its significance was that it proved that Ptolemy was not always correct, despite what other Renaissance scholars and astronomers believed. As Copernicus noted later in his masterwork *De Revolutionibus Orbium Coelestium* (On the Revolutions of the Heavenly Spheres) this astronomical observation disproved Ptolemy's belief regarding the distance of the Moon from Earth.

This one small observation would have a major impact on the history of the world. While Copernicus was not exactly sure of what this observation meant, it proved da Novara's criticism of Ptolemy to be correct. Copernicus then realized that by using scientific observation as evidence, he would no longer be bound by tradition when trying to figure out the nature of the universe.

Rome at the turn of the sixteenth century was a wellspring of art and culture. The city was the capital of the European Renaissance, and artists and thinkers from around the world gathered here. Even Copernicus was drawn to Rome during this time. Copernicus was in Rome for the great Jubilee of 1500. There he observed his first lunar eclipse and gave lectures on astronomy.

Copernicus in Rome

Eventually, Copernicus lost his financial support and he and his brother were forced to leave the university before completing their degrees. Many historians speculate this is why Copernicus left Bologna and moved to Rome. Others claim different reasons for the move. The next year, 1500, was declared a Jubilee year by Pope Alexander VI. A Jubilee year occurred every fifty years and was marked with special ceremonies and entertainment. Pilgrims would come from all over Europe to get the extra blessings that the pope and Catholic Church provided at these times. Both brothers probably wished to see the spectacle at Rome. No matter what the reason, sometime in the fall of 1500, Copernicus was in Rome.

As a twenty-seven-year-old who had come from a cosmopolitan background, Copernicus must have enjoyed all the crowds that came for the Jubilee festivals once he arrived in Rome. The city was also home to the Roman Catholic Church. Therefore, Rome was in essence the capital of Europe. The city was a breeding ground of art and ideas. Rome swelled with pilgrims, students, and visitors from around Christian Europe. Copernicus, however, was not so blinded by all the celebrations that he forgot his love of astronomy or his desire to further investigate the heavens.

Copernicus quickly established himself as a great mind, impressing both students and peers alike. Rheticus related a story of his teacher in *Narratio Prima* (First Account), published in 1540:"About the year 1500, being twenty-seven years of age more or less, [Copernicus] lectured on mathematics before a large audience of students and a throng of great men and experts in this branch of knowledge." These impressive lectures were delivered to the general public and must have contained Copernicus's general observations concerning astronomical scholarship.

Most likely, his lectures at this time did not include discussion of the heliocentric nature of the universe. From the preserved writings from the other astronomers who attended the 1500

By 1501, Copernicus was struggling with his religious beliefs and his desire for scientific exploration. With the expiration of his three-year leave of absence from his duties as canon, he ventured to Frombork, Poland, to get an extension. While in Frombork, he made several observations from the high turrets surrounding the cathedral. This was a way he could continue his scientific studies. His request was granted, and he soon returned to Padua, Italy. Today, the cathedral in Frombork *(above)* is home to a monument in honor of Copernicus.

Jubilee, there is no mention of anything about a young man expounding on heliocentricity. The idea of heliocentricity would have been a bombshell to them, proving that Copernicus had yet to devise his revolutionary system. Still, it is most likely that his lectures earned him respect from the experts in his field. They also were a way for him to keep his focus on learning despite all the distractions going on in the city.

Meanwhile, Copernicus continued to make astronomical observations. On November 6, 1500, he recorded a lunar eclipse. These first-recorded observations would eventually become pieces of a larger body of work. These first observations would help piece together one of the largest mysteries in the universe.

On the Move to Padua

The following year, Nicolaus and his brother, Andrew, went to Padua while on a leave of absence from their duties as canons in Frombork. Nicolaus Copernicus chose Padua for a practical reason—his desire to secure this leave of absence to continue studying. Since the canons did not have anyone on the staff who had any medical training to care for them if they got sick or as they aged, Copernicus told them that he wanted to learn medicine. They granted his request since they already knew that the University of Padua was a widely respected school of medicine.

Copernicus only asked for a two-year extension on his leave of absence from his work as a canon, yet a medical degree took three years to earn. Perhaps he planned on applying for another extension for the final year after he became settled in Padua. It is also possible that he had another reason to wish to

study in Padua. The city was a center of a new type of study called humanism. This field is the belief that the search for true knowledge rests on active human endeavors. In any case, Copernicus was given the extension on his leave and took up medical training at the University of Padua.

Studying the Ancient Greeks

Copernicus's studies at Padua did include a branch of knowledge that was equally important to his astronomical work and his medical training: the learning of ancient Greek. Knowledge of this language finally allowed Copernicus to examine the sources of the ancient philosophers in their original language.

This detail of a papyrus is based on work by the Greek astronomer Eudoxus of Cnidus. Eudoxus was a leading astronomer and mathematician of his day. He is best known for his early contributions toward understanding the movement of the planets. At the age of twenty-three, Eudoxus went to Athens to study at Plato's famed Academy. Eudoxus advanced many of Plato's ideas about the solar system. One of his conclusions was that Earth is at rest at a center point. Around this point, twenty-seven concentric spheres rotate. These spheres contain the Sun, the Moon, the planets, and the stars. The work of Eudoxus and other ancient Greeks would have a profound effect on Copernicus during his studies in Padua.

Here, he had the opportunity to clear up any misunderstandings that had crept in through the various translations that had been passed down over the centuries. By comparing the original ancient Greek writings to new translations, Copernicus documented mistakes in the translated versions. Copernicus needed to have the correct information on which to base his own work.

After completing two years of medical studies at Padua, he left the university and enrolled at the University of Ferrara. He did not receive a medical degree from this school, although he practiced medicine up until almost the time of his death. However, during this time, he did finally receive his doctorate in canon law. He returned to Lidzbark, Poland, to stay at the house of his uncle, Bishop Watzenrode.

CHAPTER 4

PRELUDE TO A MASTERPIECE

In 1503, with the permission of the other chapter canons, Copernicus carried out his duties while acting as his uncle's personal doctor. This arrangement allowed his uncle to include Copernicus in important political matters. Church officials were not only influential in religious matters, but they had important political roles in their communities as well. In fact, Copernicus served as his uncle's trusted adviser and confidant on numerous occasions. When, in 1508, Copernicus secured the right from the pope to two more offices that would provide him with more income for little work, it seemed as if he was on a course to become the hand-groomed successor to his aging uncle. For some reason, he never actually took the offices to which he was entitled. In 1510, he gave up his bonus as episcopal physician and left his uncle's side. He moved from Lidzbark, Poland, back to the canon chapter's headquarters in Frombork.

Why did Nicolaus Copernicus give up a promising chance at gaining a high office within the Catholic Church, and all of the influence, money, and prestige that went with it? No one

By the early 1500s, Copernicus's inner struggle between science and religion had come to a breaking point. Although he was on the verge of an illustrious career within the Catholic Church, science and the truth about the universe haunted him. Sometime in the first decade of the sixteenth century, Copernicus developed his heliocentric system. This system would first appear in his manuscript *Commentariolus* (Little Commentary). This manuscript would become the basis for his masterpiece, *De Revolutionibus Orbium Coelestium* (On the Revolutions of the Heavenly Spheres).

knows for certain, but it was also around this time that he began writing what would later come to be known as his *Commentariolus* (Little Commentary), written sometime between 1502 and 1514. Despite the uncertainty of exactly when Copernicus finished the work, what was more important was the concepts that were set down in it: namely the basic framework for a heliocentric universe. Thus, perhaps he turned away from improving a career in the church to concentrate on developing his new concept of the universe.

Copernicus most likely felt the need to put his thoughts down in writing and to have them reviewed by colleagues he respected, mainly those scholars with whom he had studied in his early career at Kraków. This is because what he was proposing was such a departure from the commonly accepted structure of the universe. Therefore, he wrote a letter detailing the conclusions that his research and thinking had brought him to and sent it to several eminent scholars. These conclusions were based on the following assumptions below, as translated by Edward Rosen, an eminent historian of astronomy:

- There is no one center of all the celestial circles or spheres.
- The center of Earth is not the center of the universe, but only of gravity and of the lunar sphere.
- All the spheres revolve about the Sun as the midpoint, and, therefore, the Sun is the center of the universe.
- The ratio of Earth's distance from Sun to the height of the firmament [this is what Copernicus called the place where the rest of the stars were in the universe] is so much smaller than the ratio of Earth's radius to its distance from the Sun that the distance from Earth to the Sun is imperceptible in comparison with the height of the firmament.
- Whatever motion appears in the firmament arises not from any motion of the firmament but from Earth's motion. The Earth together with its circumjacent elements [the air and water] performs a complete rotation on its fixed poles in a daily motion, while the firmament and highest heaven abide unchanged.

- What appear to us as motions of the Sun arise not from its motion, but from the motion of Earth and our sphere, with which we revolve about the Sun like any other planet. Earth has then more than one motion.

- The apparent retrograde and direct motion of the planets arise not from their motion but from Earth's. The motion of Earth alone, therefore, suffices to explain so many apparent inequalities in the heavens.

From these assumptions appeared, for the first time ever, a universe imagined with Earth in motion and the Sun at its center. Copernicus went on to use the knowledge he had gained from years of observations and describe why these new ideas were true, while incorporating ideas handed down from Ptolemy and the other ancient Greeks. While Copernicus did not give mathematical proofs in this first letter, he did say that he was thinking of them and would provide them in a later document. This was to be an important statement, as it showed that he continued to think about the problem and planned further work.

Copernicus never signed his name to the letter containing these seven arguments. Nor did he explain the reasons that he thought made them true. He sent it only to scholars he knew

During the late 1400s, there were many advancements in the world of astronomy. However, many instruments being used at the time had existed for centuries. The astrolabe *(top)* was used for measuring the altitudes, movements, and positions of heavenly bodies. For many centuries, it was used by astronomers and navigators alike. The celestial globe *(bottom)* was used for identifying and mapping constellations. Both of the instruments were most likely used by Copernicus and his classmates at the University of Kraków during the late fifteenth century.

BOREA SIGNA

	Longitudo		Latit			mag
borea trium	344	30		44	0	4
In sinistro brachio	347	30		17	30	4
In sinistro cubito	349	0		15	40	3
In cingulo trium australis	357	10	25	26	20	3
Media	355	10		30	0	3
Septemtrionalis trium	355	20		32	30	3
In pede sinistro	10	10		23	0	3
In dextro pede	10	30		37	20	4 Maior
Australior ab his	8	30		35	20	4 Maior
Sub poplite dextro borea	5	40		29	0	4
Austrina	5	20		28	0	4
In dextro gem	5	30		35	30	5
In syrmate sive tractu dextro borea	6	0		34	30	5
Austrina	7	30		32	30	5
A dextra manu expedes et iformis	5	0		44	0	3

Stellæ 23 et in mag tertiæ 7 quartæ et quintæ 4

Trianguli

In apice trianguli	4	20		16	30	3
In basi precedens trium	9	20		20	40	3
Media	9	30		20	20	4
Sequens trium	10	10		19	0	3

Stellæ 4 earum mag tertiæ 3 quartæ una

Igitur in ipsa septemtrionali plaga stellæ omnes 360 Magnitudinis prime 3 secunde 18 tertiæ 81 quartæ 177 quintæ 48 sextæ 13 nebulosæ i obscuræ nouem

eorum QVAE MEDIA ET CIRCA SIGNIFERVM
SVNT CIRCVLVM
ARIETIS

In cornu dextro precedens et prima omnium	0	0	bor	7	20	3 minor
Sequens in cornu	1	0	bor	8	20	3
In rictu dextro borea	4	20	bor	7	40	5

A manuscript page from Copernicus's *De Revolutionibus Orbium Coelestium*. In his groundbreaking work, Copernicus meticulously mapped out the position of heavenly bodies. This page is part of an exhaustive star catalog that notes the positions of stars in the constellations Andromeda, Triangulum, and Aries. Copernicus took his star catalog directly from the *Almagest* star catalog, which was calculated by Ptolemy around AD 150 and lists the positions of more than 1,000 stars. The *Almagest* would become the standard star catalog for more than 1,000 years. (See page 56 for an excerpt from *De Revolutionibus.*)

and trusted. He likely feared ridicule and the loss of his reputation if his work were exposed to a wide scholarly community that rejected it.

After writing and distributing the *Commentariolus* to a limited audience, Copernicus quickly realized that many of the observations he was working with were unverified. The theories put forth in the *Commentariolus* had many holes in them because they were based on ancient observations. It would take Copernicus nearly three decades to provide sufficient evidence to support his heliocentric system that would finally be revealed in his masterpiece, *De Revolutionibus Orbium Coelstium* (On the Revolutions of the Heavenly Spheres).

CHAPTER 5

Commentariolus was never published during Copernicus's lifetime, and seems to have been kept relatively private by the people to whom he sent it. Its main role was to serve as a stimulus to Copernicus's own continued thinking on the topic of the nature of the universe, even as his life as a canon in Frombork raised new challenges and distracted him. For one thing, his uncle, Bishop Watzenrode, died of illness in 1512. This must have been a deep blow to Copernicus because his uncle had looked out for him since the death of his father when he was ten.

THE IMPACT OF
DE REVOLUTIONIBUS

Another distraction from his thinking on astronomy came when the rest of the canons of his chapter selected him to be the administrator. This forced him to concentrate on managing the lands that the chapter owned. It also made him think about matters related to the value of money, and he eventually published four books on the subject.

Also, from 1519 to 1521, the Order of Teutonic Knights again tried to gain control over a large part of the kingdom of Poland. The fighting swirled around the area where Copernicus lived and was very fierce. At one point, the buildings that he lived and worked in were burned to the ground and Copernicus fled to a nearby castle. He became a leader in the resistance to the knights until a peace treaty was signed in 1521.

The Masterpiece

Despite all these distractions, Copernicus still wanted to further develop the ideas he wrote down in *Commentariolus*. Therefore, he continued to make astronomical observations of the Sun and stars. He even developed a new instrument, called a solar table, to record more information about the location of the Sun in space. This device was simply a mirror that reflected sunlight onto a wall on which he had marked lines that represented an imaginary equator for the universe. By seeing where the Sun hit these marks, Copernicus was able to better determine the time until the next equinox, the point when the length of day and night are equal. With the observations that he made with this tool and others, Copernicus began to write a new book. He called it *De Revolutionibus Orbium Coelestium* (On the Revolutions of the Heavenly Spheres).

De Revolutionibus further expanded on and refined his idea from the *Commentariolus*, in which he theorized a heliocentric universe. Copernicus kept his predecessors' idea about the perfectly circular nature of heavenly bodies' orbits, but he completely rearranged the heavenly order so that the Sun was at the center of the universe and Earth moved around it. More important, Copernicus provided plenty of tables, charts, and mathematical proofs based on his years of astronomical observations that demonstrated why his structure had to be true and Ptolemy's false. This was important because without hard scientific data and mathematical formulas, it would be impossible to convince other people that his model better explained the movement of the Sun, planets, and stars.

Historians of astronomy believe that *De Revolutionibus* took about twenty-six years to complete. While the exact date is not certain, most of them agree that it was begun sometime in 1515. By 1530, most of the work had been set down, but after spending all this time and effort, Copernicus did not yet feel that he could share his great masterpiece.

Rheticus, a young astronomer who came to study with Copernicus in 1539, finally convinced Copernicus that this great work should be published. In 1540, Rheticus published a short description, called the *Narratio Prima* (First Account), of what Copernicus planned to release. This short work was designed to generate interest for Copernicus's book and also to see whether his ideas would generate a lot of controversy. The reaction among the scholarly community seemed favorable, so Rheticus urged Copernicus to go on with his plans. By September 1541, Copernicus had finished his manuscript and sent it off to Nuremburg, Germany, to have it printed.

De Revolutionibus

De Revolutionibus was divided into six sections, or "books," each of which were further divided into chapters. The opening chapters in each book were a basic description of the idea and argument that Copernicus was going to prove. The following chapters of each book demonstrated his proofs using geometry and provided charts of his astronomical observations as supporting data. By building up his arguments in such a logical manner, Copernicus believed that he was able to prove the revolutionary proposition that he set out in *De Revolutionibus*'s preface: that

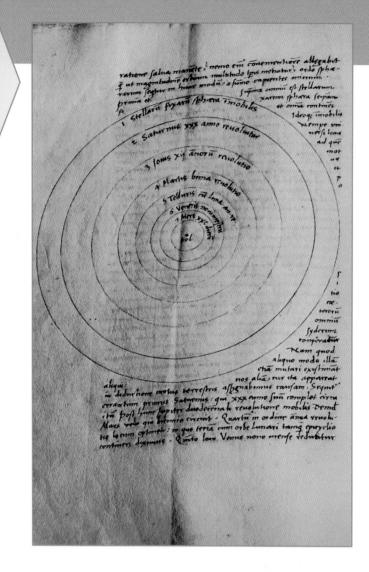

Earth moved around its own axis, while orbiting the Sun located at the center of the universe.

In the first section of *De Revolutionibus*, he set out the parts of prior astronomical learning that he believed to be true, namely that it's not true that all planetary motion is in the shape of a circle. He also agreed that ancient authorities were correct when they said that the universe was composed of interconnected spheres that held the Sun, planets, stars, and Earth. He then wrote why and how he disagreed with thinkers such as Ptolemy, Plato, and other astronomers that Earth does not move. He also included a dramatic item that he must have known would draw attention to his work: he drew a new map of the heavens. It showed the Sun sitting in the middle of the universe, surrounded by the spheres of the planets. First Mercury and then Venus circled the Sun. Next came Earth, and then Mars, Jupiter, and Saturn in the next to last circle. Finally came the sphere holding the stars. For the first time in print, people could see that Earth no longer held the primary place in the universe, but was just another planet like the others.

In the second section of *De Revolutionibus*, Copernicus described the geometry of circles that he believed helped prove this radical change from accepted thought. In the third and fourth sections of *De Revolutionibus*, he showed how his idea gave greater accuracy to predicting the solar equinoxes and solstices. In the last two sections, he provided the mathematical formulas that more accurately described the motions of the five planets. At every point throughout the *De Revolutionibus*, he provided tables of the observations he had made during his long career so that other scholars could check his reasoning. He wanted educated people and scholars to accept his reasoning, and he believed that his careful mathematical analysis linked to the data that it was based on would win them over.

After completing *De Revolutionibus*, Copernicus was worried that religious authorities, especially Pope Paul III, might condemn him for the contents of his book once it was published. In an effort to gain the favor of the Catholic Church, he wrote a special preface and dedication to the pope to be included with the book's main body. In this preface, Copernicus acknowledged that some would attack him for what he has written, but he published his book because he believed it would be of some use to the church as a means of producing a better calendar. This was an important goal of the Catholic Church

THE REFORMATION

In 1517, a Catholic priest named Martin Luther nailed to the door of a church in Wittenberg, Germany, a list of ninety-five things that he thought the church needed to fix. These arguments, or theses, were so divisive that eventually the Catholic Church excommunicated Martin Luther as a heretic. However, Luther had gained so many followers all across western Europe that when he was forced out, they decided to follow him and form a new church. Known as the Protestant Reformation, this would be the start of a series of breaks that would slowly erode the power of the Catholic Church over politics, culture, and religion throughout western Europe.

Nicolaus Copernicus was not the only one challenging the Catholic Church during the early sixteenth century. The Reformation, which began in 1517, was one of the most important turning points in European history. The very foundation of the Catholic Church shook when the Reformation created the split of European Christians into Protestants and Catholics.

because it wanted to have an accurate calendar to precisely mark holy days such as Easter. Copernicus hoped that by giving a practical application for his efforts, he could keep from being denounced by those in the church who thought his work was blasphemous. Unfortunately, he did not need to worry about such matters for long. His book was published sometime at the end of March 1543, and he died on May 24, 1543. Despite the many legends that have spread throughout the centuries, he never saw a copy of his finished printed work.

Consequences of Copernicus's Work

Copernicus's book was rejected by most religious leaders as being heretical and a direct threat to scripture. This occurred despite Copernicus's blatant attempts to win the pope's favor and his student Rheticus's similar attempts to gain the approval of Martin Luther and the leaders of the Protestant Reformation.

Shortly after Copernicus's death, the Catholic Church began to tighten its grip on the intellectual pursuits of Europe. By 1616, the church had formally banned Copernicus's work. Astronomers, however, could not ignore *De Revolutionibus* because of the detailed mathematical proofs and charts of observations that Copernicus had included to support his conclusions. For example, Tycho Brahe (1546–1601) was a Danish astronomer employed by the king of Denmark to see if Copernicus was correct. In order to do this, Brahe realized he, too, would need to spend years making accurate astronomical observations. He improved on the existing instruments needed to make these observations and created what is now considered the first true astronomical observatory. Because of his religious convictions, Brahe could not accept Copernicus's heliocentric

In 1632, Italian astronomer, physicist, and philosopher Galileo Galilei published the *Dialogo Sopra i Due Massimi Sistemi del Mondo, Tolemaico e Copernicano* (Dialogue Concerning the Two Chief World Systems, Ptolemaic and Copernican). The work would give the Copernican system its much-deserved credibility. During Galileo's age, the Catholic Church held strong to the belief that Earth is the center of the universe. Galileo was allowed to write about the Copernican system, but only if he treated Copernicus's ideas as theory, not fact. In response, Galileo wrote *Dialogo* as a conversation between a layman and two philosophers, one subscribing to Copernicus's beliefs, the other to Ptolemy's. But once *Dialogo* reached the public, Galileo was condemned by the church and sentenced to house arrest.

system. However, because Brahe needed data to refute Copernicus, the rigorous astronomical observations he made in an attempt to disprove Copernicus would be used by a later astronomer to actually support Copernicus's ideas.

While Brahe could not accept a sun-centered universe, his assistant Johannes Kepler (1571–1630) could. Brahe had hired Kepler to help him record and interpret all the information from his nightly observations. Using this information and Copernicus's model for a starting point, Kepler tried to disprove the counter-arguments to Copernicus that Brahe had. Kepler realized that Copernicus was correct in writing that Earth moved around the Sun, but wrong in thinking that this movement was in a circle. Kepler figured out that Earth really moved in an ellipse around the Sun, and so did the other planets. By using Copernicus's work as a stepping-stone, he discovered the three laws of planetary motion that are still used today by astronomers.

Galileo Galilei

Galileo Galilei (1564–1642) was another scientist who took the ideas of Copernicus as the basis for his own work. Because he wished to prove Copernicus correct, Galileo developed a vastly improved telescope, which allowed him to make even more accurate observations. Using this device, he discovered that Venus was closer to the Sun than to Earth, observations that supported the heliocentric system. Galileo continued to make observations and developed many ideas about gravity and how forces work, which further refined and expanded the Copernican system of the universe. However, nearly 150 years after Copernicus challenged the beliefs set forth by the Catholic Church, Galileo would share a similar fate. Although Galileo proved without a doubt the authenticity of Copernicus's helio-centric theory, he was condemned by the Catholic Church and placed under house arrest, where he eventually died.

The writings of both Kepler and Galileo became widely dis-tributed among the growing scientific community. Because both of them were able to blend mathematical solutions to increasingly accurate observations, it became harder and

The courage of Copernicus changed the world forever. It was his desire to seek the truth and his challenging of authority that would inspire great minds for centuries to come. During his lifetime, Copernicus received little acclaim for his groundbreaking work. It would take centuries for Copernicus to be recognized for his contributions to science and for laying the groundwork for modern astronomy. Many monuments now stand in his honor, including this one in his hometown in Torun, Poland.

harder for critics to deny the truth of their work and the foundation upon which it was built: the heliocentric universe of Nicolaus Copernicus.

Conclusion

Four hundred years after the publication of his masterpiece, Nicolaus Copernicus finally got the widespread public acclaim that was due to him. In 1943, a great celebration was held on the 400th anniversary of the printing of Copernicus's *De Revolutionibus*. Despite all the trials and horrors caused by World War II (1939–1945), United States President Franklin D. Roosevelt took a break from running the war effort to participate in these events. Roosevelt, along with countless scholars and foreign dignitaries, wanted to highlight the importance of Copernicus's scholarship to our understanding of the universe in which we live. The celebration included radio plays dramatizing his discoveries, speeches, and dedications of plaques and memorials. All these tributes emphasized that it was Nicolaus Copernicus's courage to seek out the truth and share it with others that created a new way for humans to understand their place in the universe. By putting the Sun in its proper place and showing that Earth moved, Copernicus created the foundations of modern astronomy. Without his work, the later scientific discoveries that led to the astronauts' trip to the Moon, the Hubble telescope, and even cable television (which depends on satellites transmitting signals from orbit) would not have been possible.

INDEX

Credits

About the Author

Josh Sakolsky is a freelance writer in and around New York City. He currently lives in New Jersey with his wife Stacy and their "kids" Hydra and Thumper.

Editor: Charles Hofer; Photo Researcher: Jeffrey Wendt